States of Matter

Density

by Rebecca Pettiford

Bullfrog Books

Ideas for Parents and Teachers

Bullfrog Books let children practice reading informational text at the earliest reading levels. Repetition, familiar words, and photo labels support early readers.

Before Reading
- Discuss the cover photo. What does it tell them?
- Look at the picture glossary together. Read and discuss the words.

During Reading
- "Walk" through the book with the reader. Discuss new or unfamiliar words. Sound them out together.
- Look at the photos together. Point out the photo labels.

After Reading
- Prompt the child to think more. Ask: Experiment with water and objects. Which objects float? Which ones sink?

Bullfrog Books are published by Jump!
5357 Penn Avenue South
Minneapolis, MN 55419
www.jumplibrary.com

Copyright © 2026 Jump! International copyright reserved in all countries. No part of this book may be reproduced in any form without written permission from the publisher.

Jump! is a division of FlutterBee Education Group.

Library of Congress Cataloging-in-Publication Data is available at www.loc.gov or upon request from the publisher.

ISBN: 979-8-89213-966-3 (hardcover)
ISBN: 979-8-89213-967-0 (paperback)
ISBN: 979-8-89213-968-7 (ebook)

Editor: Jenna Gleisner
Designer: Anna Peterson

Photo Credits: alistaircotton/iStock, cover (duck); Litvalifa/Shutterstock, cover (rock); New Africa/Shutterstock, 1; on_france/Shutterstock, 3; Shot what you like/iStock, 4 (rock), 5 (rock), 6–7 (rock), 23br (rock); CJ Stevenson/Shutterstock, 5 (fish); Shutterstock, 4 (background), 5 (background), 6–7 (background), 23br (background); pavlemarjanovic/iStock, 8–9 (ball), 23tr (ball); nemke/iStock, 8–9 (background), 23tr (background); pamela_d_mcadams/iStock, 10; roman_sh/iStock, 11; bosenok/iStock, 12–13; Grafissimo/iStock, 14–15; Pat_Hastings/Shutterstock, 16–17; Pat_Hastings/iStock, 18–19; Carolyn Franks/Shutterstock, 20–21 (bobber); MirekKijewski/iStock, 20–21 (worm); Shutterstock, 20–21 (background); Andrey Eremin/Shutterstock, 22 (oil); Pavel Aleks/Shutterstock, 22 (jar); bl0ndie/iStock, 24.

Printed in the United States of America at Corporate Graphics in North Mankato, Minnesota.

Table of Contents

Sink or Float?	4
Oil and Water	22
Picture Glossary	23
Index	24
To Learn More	24

Sink or Float?

A rock **sinks**.

It goes to the bottom.
Why?

Everything is made of **particles**.

A rock has a lot.

They are packed tight.

The rock is **denser** than water.

rock particles

air particles

A beach ball **floats**.

Why?

It is full of air.

Water is denser.

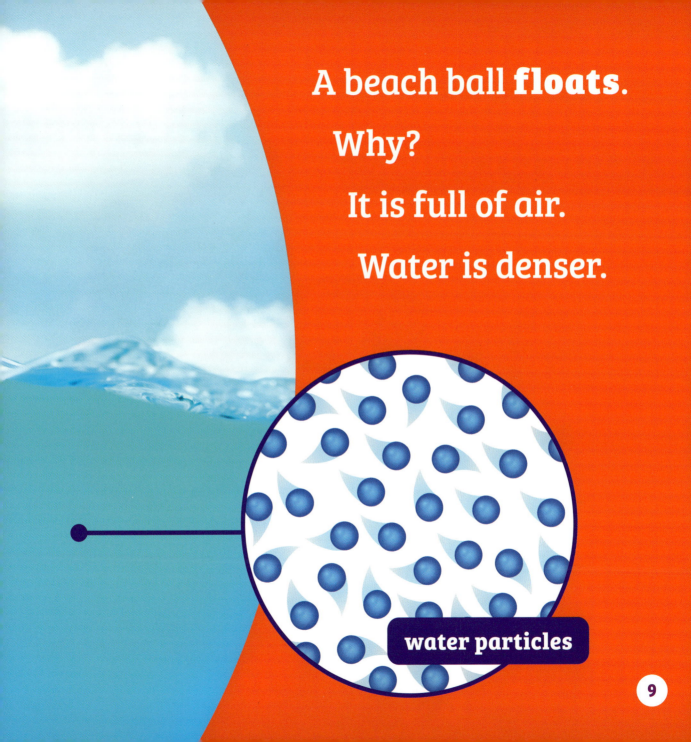

water particles

Metal is denser. Coins are metal.

coin

They sink.

A ship is big.

It is heavy.

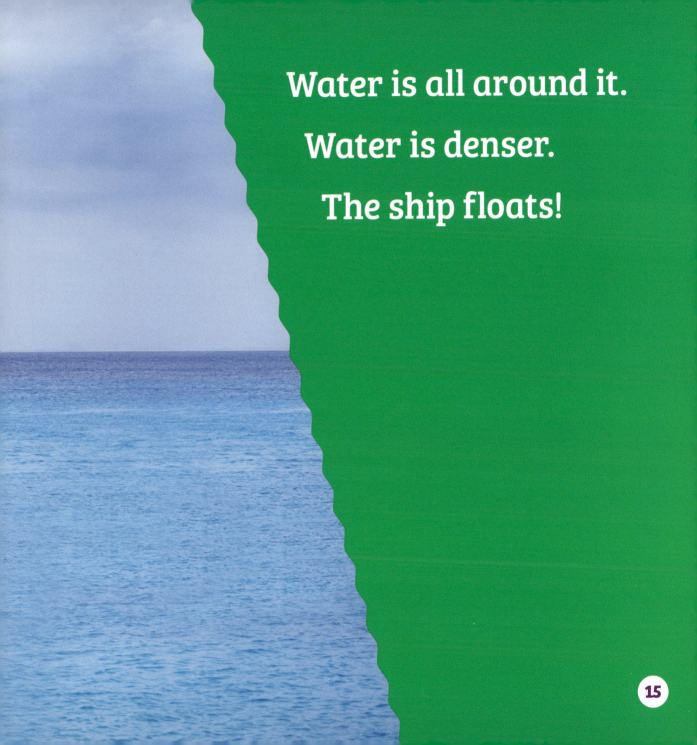

Water is all around it.
Water is denser.
The ship floats!

An egg sinks.

It is denser than water.

We add salt.
Look! The egg floats!
Why?
Saltwater is denser.

Let's try more!
Does it sink or float?

Oil and Water

Which is denser? Oil or water? Let's find out!

What You Need:
- clear glass jar
- water
- spoon
- tablespoon
- cooking oil

Steps:
1. Fill the jar about half full with water.
2. Measure and pour four tablespoons (60 milliliters) of oil into the jar.
3. Mix and wait.

What happens to the oil?
Does it sink or float?

Oil is less dense than water. It floats!

Picture Glossary

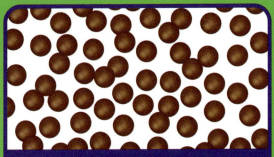

denser
More dense, or having more particles with little space between them. Density is a measure of how heavy or light an object is for its size.

floats
Rests on top of water.

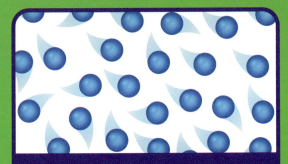

particles
Extremely small pieces of something.

sinks
Goes below the surface of water.

Index

air 9
beach ball 9
bottom 5
coins 10
egg 16, 19
floats 9, 15, 19, 20
particles 6
rock 4, 6
salt 19
ship 12, 15
sinks 4, 11, 16, 20
water 6, 9, 15, 16

To Learn More

Finding more information is as easy as 1, 2, 3.

❶ Go to **www.factsurfer.com**

❷ Enter **"density"** into the search box.

❸ Choose your book to see a list of websites.